Get

Your

Dream Job

Today

Jonathan O. Olukotun

ISBN: **978-1512108088**

DEDICATION

This book is lovingly dedicated to youths world-wide, who are passionately making an impact in their world for the betterment of mankind.

FOREWORD

To start with, *I'm not in this book promising you a get rich Quick plan*, or what you will achieve over-night.

What I have outlined here are things that If you carry out consistently, will with time create a gradual stream of income for you. The steps outlined here are things countless number of people are using to earn a livelihood. *Those who are looking for a get rich quick scheme most often end up in hands of scammers which are rife on the world wide web, who 'rip them off'.* Real wealth takes time to build up, **with just a few exceptions**.

To convince yourself, do a search on the web to prove for yourself that what I have written are facts.

With the Economic meltdown that is upon us globally in this twenty-first century

Earning a living becomes increasingly challenging

The few white-collar jobs that are available if being completed for by thousands of Graduates being milled out of Universities and Other higher institutions of learning: the competition is becoming stiffer for Degree holders.

To make matter worse, if you have this desire to upgrade your educational status by studying for a second degree, the cost is quite overwheming especially for a jobless person.

Is there any hope for you?

Yes there sure is...

I am here offering you hope.

Have you ever thought of doing the job you love most...job that fit your Skills and much more job that you can do at your location,pace and time?Look no further...

By the time you read through this book and put into practice what you will find therein...you definitely are on your way to earning yourself a Job...Today

I am not here offering you opportunity like so many fraudulent guys on the web that give promise of earning a fortune over night.

What I'm going to be directing you to is what will gradually position you to starting an honest livelihood that will grow your earning power over time.

The good news is also that I am not telling you something I'm not familiar with. I am actually actively involved in working on these platforms.

So then let me hold your hand and guide you through the process.

Jonathan O. Olukotun
email-jolukotun@icthelpsdesk.com
Website-http://www.icthelpsdesk.com/

CONTENTS

ACKNOWLEDGMENTS

I wish to specially appreciate my dear wife Josephine Nwakego Olukotun and my Children Jesimiel, Jathniel and Tofunmi-my team members; for all their support. Thanks a million.

I also wish to acknowledge all who have motivated me towards success in one way or the other especially through their books:-Dr. Mike Murdock, John Mason, Dr. John Avanzini, Dr. Miles Munroe (Of blessed memory) and lots of other great Men and Women too numerous to mention here. You labor is yielding results.

I say to you all, God bless you real good. Please insure you fulfill your destiny

CHAPTER ONE

Getting Started

To start up, you need to decide on the

1. Type of Job that you want.

2. The time you are willing to commit to the job you need. Do you need a full time job or a part time Job?

To assist you in this respect, you need to come to terms with what Skills you have.

There is no person on this planet that cannot do anything...what skills do you have? Writing, Typing, reading, technical skills etc. I have seen physically challenged people doing some astounding things..like Singing, Writing, answering Phone calls etc. You may want to itemise them by writing them on a piece of paper.

What form of education do you have?

The moment you start itemising those things, the more you realise that you have something to offer to the World: that could earn you a livelihood.

In this our day....the quickest jobs to get are online jobs. Therefore the series of jobs I'm introducing to you in this edition of my book are online jobs . I will get to more details later.

You will need:-

1. A laptop. Laptops are cheap these days-You can get a netbook for about $230. (*My advice..if you can get a friend's pc or Laptop to use for a while until you start making money that will be fine*)

2. An internet modem-To enable you connect to the internet.

3. A head-piece (That will enable you communicate on the web with less noise from the environment)

4. You will need a quiet location where you can work without distraction.

CHAPTER TWO

Job Opportunities

Numerous job opportunities abound around that are available to those who take time to look around.

The advent of the World wide Web in the 21st century has opened to us a new world view and operation. The World has become a global village.

It is now possible to have an online office with your staff spread across . You could have your Manager in the US, while your secretary is located in Croatia and your accountant located in India. This is made possible by Platforms like Elanceor Odesk, which provide a staffing platform where Employers from around the World are connected with Contractors (Workers).

The first job opportunity I'm recommending in this book to you is available in

Work at Home – www.elance.com/ or www.odesk.com.

As of the time of publishing this book, there merger between Odesk and Elancehas been completed, and the new name is now **www.upwork.com/**

I am registered with both and has also worked for Employers on both Platforms.

There so many kinds of jobs being advertised daily, ranging from Data Entry, Virtual assistant, Technical Support, Article Writing, Internet research, Trasncription etc.

I will be taking you through the process of getting a job in any of the Platforms.

It is quite simple to get started working on any of these platforms.

Register

To register is quite simple. All you need is a valid email address. You are provided with a registration form which you are required to fill and submit. To register for either Elanceor Odesk is free.

After registration, you are required to confirm your registration using the email address that you registered with. Once you do that, you are on.

The next step after this is to complete your online profile. This includes, Uploading your profile picture, Filling in your location, Address (The address must indicate where you are located physically, which can be verified. People that deal with you want to know that you are a Real person with a verifiable address), Educational Qualification, your work experience etc.. Your completing these will make you more likely to get a Job. You will also be asked to include your minimum hourly price-a general minimumamount you can accept to work per hour.

Tip- *I need to advice at this point that you should be willing to give a very low amount, until your popularity has been boosted on the platform.*

1.   Readiness Test. For the two platforms you are required to take readiness test. This is to ensure you arefamiliar with their platform and ready to work. Instruction materials are available on each site to guide you and prepare you for the test. For oDesk, the test is Odesk readiness Test. For each of this test your are expected to pass 100%. If you do not pass the first time, you are allowed to rewrite immediately.

2.   Take more test. Under each of the platforms, Skills Tests are available for you to take to prove to you prospective Employers that you actually have the required skills. *The more Skill tests that you take, the better your chances of getting jobs quicker.*

Getting your first Job on Elanceor oDesk.

Now that you have completed your profile, passed the readiness test and also taken a few skill tests, you are ready to apply for your first Job.

Usually you can browse for jobs by typing a keyword that will enable you to search specifically or just browse for all the jobs available on the platform. The list will usually be displayed.

It is best apply for jobs for which you are best skilled at this initial time.

In applying, you usually should outline out Skills as applied in carrying out previous Jobs. Make it as brief as possible but enough to sell yourself to your prospective employer.

In Elancetoo, you are required to outline your approach to the job. Using your past job experiences outline your procedure for carry out your jobs e.g how will you carry out your trouble-shooting procedure if it is an IT issue.

On Elance, you can preview, make corrections before submitting your Proposal.

Some criteria Employers look for in offering you a job include, Your experience, your pricing. Some employer are willing to pay a high price if in their judgement you have the experience they need.

The Interview Process

The interview process is usually online, through one of the chatting applications. The most popular one is Skype. It can be either messaging, Audio or Video. I have had interviews for jobs using all the three. At a time, I was require to share my screen through Skype so my interviewer could view what I was doing on the Screen.

Tips towards a successful interview

I. Be available at least 15 minutes to your interview and inform your interviewer of your availability.

II. Be sincere about you claims.

III. Sell yourself by focusing on your area of strength.

IV. If you will not be available for interview, inform your interviewer well ahead of time and seek for a new schedule.

2. Online Advertisement / Marketing

This is another job opportunity that is growing by the day. A lot of organisation are taking advantage of the world-wide reach of the internet to advertise their products. I will mention a few that I know.

You usually will register with such organisation as an Affiliate. Some will require that you have a website before you are registered as an affiliate. Others will allow you to advertise their products using any means that you choose either through Blogs, Letters, Forums like facebook. When you register, you are given a link to their site /products which is unique for each affiliate. *Whenever anybody clicks on such a link that leads them to buy a product from their Site, you are paid a commission.* One of those sites where I have been paid commission severally, and which I'm recommending to you is

-> www.hostgator.com/

To register as an affiliate, click on the Affiliates link and fill in the required information.

To enable you do this you will need a working email address, which you must confirm to complete your registration Process.

How to drive traffic to your site.

Hostgator usually will also provide you with banners to paste on your website to market their products.

Other Organisations you can register with and market their products to earn commission are:-

1. www.bluesnap.com/

2. www.amazon.com/

3. Linkshare.com/

4. Commission Junction

Many others are available. You can check this out through www.google.com

There are several ways of driving traffic to you site. I will only mention a few.

A. Register your website with search engines like www.google.com

B.   Join forums like Facebook and Twitter then create alink there that will lead people to you website.

C.   Put banners ofpopular sites on your website, so that when people search the web, they will be directed to your Site.

3. Website Marketing

This time around, you are taking your affilate marketing to a new level. You decide to have a website. To own a website is not too expensive.

What you need?

A. A unique name. You need to decide on a name that will help to market your product. You will need to register this name.Domain names are quite cheap, and at the time of writing this book is about $10. This name is refered to as you Domain name. It will be something like this www.yourName.com

There are many types of extensions you may use, but the most popular for business is .com. .org is for organisations.

With the purchase of a domain name, you also need to pay for a hosting plan. You can get one of this from a hosting company. One of which i have introduced you to before :- www.hostgator.com/

When you have purchased your domain name and have a hosting plan, then you need a website designed for you. Websites vary from basic and very simple to very complex and expensive ones. If you so wish I could develop a cost effective website for you.

Once your website is up and running, all you need to do is to keep updating it with things to advertise to the World fromCompanies you are advertising for.

5. eBooks Writing

The last type of job opportunity I will be challenging you to consider is e-book writing and Selling.

You might be almost saying out aloud...eBook! I am not an Author....

Come on....everybody has a story to tell...Surely you can do something!

eBooks can be written on almost anything. Surely, you have information that can be of benefit to somebody in this world...Health Tips, Food recipe', Study guide...the list is endless. Just put it together.

Don't know how to write ebooks? I will give you links of material that could be of help. On the Other hand, if you need my assistance, I am available to consult for you.

Send me a mail at jolukotun@icthelpsdesk.com

If you on the other hand decide to dive in yourself, these materials could be of help.

http://www.pcworld.com/article/253618/how_to_use_microso ft_word_to_create_an_ebook.html

https://liber.io/

CHAPTER THREE

How to receive your payments

Receiving your payments online is now much easier than in the past. There are several options I will be outlining in this book.

1.   Paypal

Paypal is a payment processing organisation that enable you to receive and send money across the globe. They are the most popular payment processing outfit, but not operate in some Countries. They just began operation in Nigeria in year 2014.

All you need to do is register for free with them using a valid email address. Once you confirm your email address, you are good to go. You usually connect your credit card or Dom Bank account to your Paypal Account. For assisting you in receiving payment for you, Paypal usually charges a fee.

1. MasterCard Payment

This is the most effective means of receiving payment online that I know about. One Organisation that operates this is *www.Payoneer.com/* Once you register with

Payoneer, you can apply for their master card, customized for you. Sometimes, it is customized for the organisation you work for. I have personally received two of such cards. The good thing, is that it is free of charge. It took about two weeks to receive my card in Warri, Nigeria. Payoneer Card is a favoured payment processing option for International Workers on Odesk and Elance. Once you have received your card, you need to set your payment option on oDesk and Elanceto the Card. Your fund is loaded on the Card, then your can receive it in your Local Currency from an Automated Teller Machine (ATM) in your Country.

2. Cheque

Some organisation Pay their workers through cheque You usually must have a Domicilliary Account to pay in such check.

Tip!- *Apart from using the services of www.payoneer.com/ to process your payment, you also an opportunity as on of their account holder to refer people to them and earn $25 for each referral that registers and uses their account and receives a minimum of $100 for the first payment.*

CHAPTER FOUR

Conclusion

To conclude, There is still so much to say about getting the job you desire, but I will leave the rest to the Second Edition of this Book. The most important last message I want to leave with you, is that you should start Today!

A Chinese Proverb goes thus:-

"The journey of a thousand miles begins with one step"

– Lao Tzu

If you do not start today while the Vision is hot in your heart, by the time you wake up tommorow morning, you may start rationalizing why it may not be possible, or you may encounter distractions.

For more information send me an email:jolukotun@icthelpsdesk.com

Thanks for reading my Book. It will be a great joy to me, to hear and celebrate with you your success Story.

*Watch out for the Second Edition and my second Book-'**How to Start Your Business From Zero Level** And Succeed'*

Best Regards

-Jonathan O. Olukotun-

jolukotun@icthelpsdesk.com

ABOUT THE AUTHOR

Jonathan Olorunleke Olukotun is a Nigerian who has passion for motivating business Start-ups. He is a Software Developer and Systems Integrator. A graduate of Electronics and Communication Engineering, he is also the CEO of Classic Solutions Nigeria, a company that is specialized in developing customizable Software Solutions, Systems Integration and Support. Popular among their Products are: Classic Solutions Smart Store and Classic Solutions Payroll System.
E-mail:-jolukotun@icthelpsdesk.com
Website: www.icthelpsdesk.com/

www.ingramcontent.com/pod-product-compliance
Lightning Source LLC
Chambersburg PA
CBHW070758180526
45168CB00004B/1668